THE *Words* THAT THOU GAVEST ME

ROBYN SORENSEN

ISBN 978-1-68526-912-8 (Paperback)
ISBN 978-1-68526-913-5 (Digital)

Covenant Books
11661 Hwy 707
Murrells Inlet, SC 29576
www.covenantbooks.com

I AM SIMON

What if your name was Simon and they pulled you from the crowd
Uncertain of what was happening, for the shouts were far too loud?
And as they brought you closer, for words, you were at a loss
And now you stood right next to Him, compelled to bear his cross
Who was this man of suffering, so badly beaten He could barely stand?
And why would anyone pick you to lend a helping hand?
The sight before you wrenched your heart, and you didn't know what
to do
So you lifted the cross that you didn't understand—it had now
become your burden too
You could see the hill before you. The path was long and hard
How would He ever make it, so beaten, bruised, and marred?
The spit that was aimed at Him, it now had hit you too
And the cursing stung your ear—could these accusations be true?
What did He do to deserve all this? You simply couldn't imagine
For this was unlike anything that you could ever fathom
The anger and the hatred, so vehemently displayed, made you wonder,
Is this the King whom everyone betrayed?
And so you whispered, "Jesus, it's not much further now
I am here to help you. We'll get through somehow"
As He lifted His bloodstained face, I knew in my heart it was true
That this indeed was the King of the world
As He said, "I did this for you"

TURN YOUR EAR
TO HEAVEN

A people stressed and burdened
It wasn't meant to be this way
So I turn my ear to heaven
Lord Jesus, what do you say?
A weary worn-out people
Burning out at record pace
We really don't know how
To slow down and enter grace
But if we listen and apply
All that He does say
It's then we can enter into rest
And the chaos goes away
For when you're standing in the truth
The world can't help but see
That there's a peace, a calm, a difference
A blood-bought victory

SURRENDER

Some broken, some hurting, some lost
Amid life's storms we are tossed
Back and forth, to and fro
Deeper and deeper and deeper we go
Holding our breath, we search for fresh air
Wondering how we ever got here
The truth that we knew but a distant thought
Whose we are, seems we forgot
The lies that we buy into each day
As the enemy continues to lead us astray
But the God whom we know still beckoning too
Still extending His hand to pull us through
Says we are not too far from the way back home
For in Christ Jesus we are never alone
He will lead if we follow—the choice is yours
Along the way, many roads, many doors
Straight is His gate and narrow the way
And few there be who find it today
You must seek and desire with a whole heart and soul
Let go of the world; give the Holy Spirit control
And soon you will find true healing begin
Surrender it all and let Jesus back in

THE EMPTY TOMB

This Holy Week, as I reflect
At the tomb I found everything I didn't expect
As a Christian, I knew no body was there
He was risen, ascended, caught up in the air
So just what was it I'd expect to find
As the story of Easter began to unwind
Well, first off, Easter's not a once-a-year thing
I could meet my risen Jesus every morning
And although the tomb was empty, I would not be
For He sent His Holy Spirit to indwell me
And at the tomb, where one would shed tears
Mine would be washed away, along with my fears
When I gazed in the empty tomb, I saw myself
It was me, in the pages of that Bible on my shelf
As I gazed at the empty tomb, I saw Jesus suffering
And I realized that I'm the one who lives like a king
As I thought of the treasures that He left behind
At the empty tomb, I realized now they're all mine
As I gazed into the empty tomb, I saw a tree where Jesus hung
Unlike all the other trees, different was this one
And in the empty tomb, this tree stood alone
And there hung my God—I was chilled to the bone
As I gazed into the empty tomb, on the floor His robe lay
Everything that He bore, He bore for me on that day
As I gazed into the empty tomb, I could hear all the mocking
And I wondered how many I have hurt while talking
As I gazed into the empty tomb, I was stunned by the silence
Realizing He spoke not a word while enduring the violence

As I gazed into the empty tomb, it was as black as the night
Not seeing a thing, I saw Jesus, my light
As I gazed into the empty tomb, I saw His stripes, felt His pain
Then I saw in my life all the healing that came
As I gazed into the empty tomb, where He died among His own creation
I saw His death, my life, my salvation
As I gazed into the empty tomb, it was filled for me that day
How many others would come to know that empty tomb that made the way
So as you gaze into that empty tomb, to you comes a decision
Will you receive the Father's gift, a Savior who has risen?

WHAT HAVE YOU BEEN TAUGHT

We have been taught wrong, in the name of "to belong"
We have bought into sin, in the name of "to fit in"
We have been taught there are many ways
Instead of what the Bible says
We have been taught that whatever we believe is true
Instead of what Jesus has done for you
We have been taught that it is "all about me"
Instead of the Savior on that tree
Many churches teach of a worldly love
Instead of true love that came down from above
We have all been taught to "not offend"
Instead of what really happens in the end
No matter what it is that you've been taught
There is a holy God, and we've been blood-bought

IN TWENTY-FOUR HOURS

I live in a twenty-four-hour town, where people are always putting us down
Oh yes, there's sin around the clock, but let us have a little talk
While we take a look at others' sins, let's not forget where we have been
And in twenty-four hours I have found where there is sin, more grace to abound
Yes, gambling and drinking everywhere, but twenty-four hours there is also prayer
When the darkness of sin takes cover at night, twenty-four hours someone shines Jesus's light
Oh, the billboards that glorify women and sex, twenty-four hours people repent, because of their effects
The carousing and cheating that break our families down, twenty-four hours a day can be found in any other town
The stealing and the lies that we do to feed our sin, twenty-four hours on many corners is a church to enter in
Sin at any time to God is not pleasing, so twenty-four hours a day I keep on believing
I believe for the lost in this city of sin, twenty-four hours a day, in Jesus's name, for victory again
And twenty-four hours of a lifestyle that isn't right, twenty-four hours there are those who for the good do fight
Sin twenty-four hours a day from any city will not depart, because sin is a twenty-four-hour sickness of the heart
And that, my friend, is why the Lord Jesus came, not to call our cities but, twenty-four hours a day, each one of us by name

CHRISTMAS STILL

Through all the season it is hard to be still
As I focus my intention to follow God's will
A babe in a manger, born on the hay
A most relevant occasion that we call Christmas Day
We've become busy people as we bustle around
Where a silent night can hardly be found
And the pressures of the season are worn on the face
Instead of the true meaning of God's amazing grace
Oh, the financial burdens find that our spirit won't lift
With hearts often heavy searching out our next gift
Oh, the cash and the credit from our spending spree
Often replace the true meaning of His gift that came free
The food and the goodies and traditions passed down
Can't compare to the true Bread of Life the shepherds found
As we celebrate and ponder o'er this holy night
Do you feel in your spirit something not quite right?
Slow down, take a break, and pause through your day
Know that Christmas is a Savior—He's our hope and He's The Way
If you don't have peace and wonder if you ever will
Seek out a silent night, for you need Christmas still

FISHERWOMAN

I am a fisherwoman, though I've never touched a pole
I stand ashore life's ocean, casting for one's soul
That the lost may be reeled in and put on solid ground
Safe in the arms of Jesus from crashing waves all around
I've never used a worm—no, that's not been my bait
I've used the Gospel truth, to tell of a lost man's fate
I've never had a license that expired or needed renewed
I tell of man's salvation and God's Word that's sure and true
I'm never kept from fishing by bad weather in the morn
I am called to do the fishing that can weather any storm
So morning, noon, or night, I'll fish right where I'm at
I am God's fisherwoman—will you be His next catch?

NO MATTER WHAT

No matter what the trial may be
No matter what His call
No matter what this life does bring
My Savior sees me through it all
The world can seem so harsh at times
Like a love song gone awry
Its tenderness has turned to stone
And like a love song makes you cry
So I look beyond my natural eye
It's only then that I can see
Heaven sings a greater song
It's called eternity
Sweeter than any love song
That I have ever heard
Angelic voices singing out
Our God's unfailing Word
It flows to me through promises
Of truth and righteousness
It straightens out the sinner's life
So often made a mess
It strengthens even the weakest
Giving hope afresh and anew
It gives true meaning to one's life
Something this world could never do

HE IS THE WAY

The struggle that goes on in you, I really understand
It makes me want to come to you and take you by the hand
To let you know a better way is waiting there for you
If you would only trust in God—He longs to see you through
There is nothing that's too hard for Him or out of His control
But you must choose to surrender all, from deep within your soul
For He's a God of second chances, with blessings that await
So don't believe in Satan's lies—addiction's not your fate
You must let go and rise above these things that keep you down
Put your trust in Jesus Christ. Then you're on solid ground
And when you do, it's then you'll see the lies and the deceit
That come from the one whose lifelong goal is bringing us defeat
And that is why I'm telling you these things I know for sure
Jesus stands and waits for you—He's knocking at your door
By now I hope that you can see I truly understand
All you really need to do is take hold of Jesus's hand
For God has put Satan in his place two thousand years ago
He did it once for you and me, and this is how I know
He sent our Savior, Jesus Christ, His one and only Son
And your victory over any drug, well, it's already won

EYES ON HIM

When things go wrong and nothing is clear and life's situations fill
you with fear
You gotta keep your eyes on Him
When your heart is breaking and sadness holds tight and it doesn't
seem things will ever be right
You gotta keep your eyes on Him
When sickness has struck and your body is weak and you can't
remember when things were so bleak
You gotta keep your eyes on Him
When anger is raging and you want to lash out and you are filled
with hatred, worry, and doubt
You gotta keep your eyes on Him
When life gets busy and your days fill with stress and all you would
like is peace and rest
You gotta keep your eyes on Him
When your money won't stretch as far as you need and there is not
enough food for the mouths you must feed
You gotta keep your eyes on Him
When there is no one around and you haven't a friend and it seems
lonely nights might never end
You gotta keep your eyes on Him
When drugs are your answer and you'd like one more drink because
they ease all your problems, or so you think
You gotta keep your eyes on Him
'Cause when your time's up and it's your time to go
And you hear Him calling, only then will you know
That you kept your eyes on Him

CHRISTMAS SURPRISE

Christmas is that time of year
Folks are friendly and filled with cheer
Putting aside meanness and greed
Reaching out to those in need
The traffic gets heavy, the parking absurd
All over town Christmas songs can be heard
The stores are all open with bargains galore
As shelves are emptying all over the store
People rush to choose that perfect tree
Light and decorate it for all to see
The house full of goodies and all Mom's baking
Decisions and plans, families are making
But through the excitement and joy of the season
Have you thought about the one true reason?
The Savior who was given for you and for me
He came to forgive and to set us free
And I hope come Christmas Day you'll see
This gift can't be wrapped or put under a tree
You don't have to worry if it's in your price range
And it's for sure a gift you won't want to exchange

OUR TRUE PHYSICIAN

It's amazing to see when I look all around
Illnesses, diseases, tearing us down
Do this. Take that. Come back in a week
Oh, the things that we hear from the doctors we seek
But we must not forget it's not man whom we need
It's not medications on which we need to feed
It is through God's Word and trust in the Lord
Faith in Jesus, to truly be cured
It is not operations that make us right
It's not by our own power or might
It's God who has a hand in it all
We must lean on Him if we don't want to fall
It's to Jesus our illnesses we must yield
And remember that it's by His stripes we were healed

ABIDING IN CHRIST

Daily walking with Jesus is the way it should be
For the devil lurks, deceitful, crafty
In God's Word and in prayer we must stay
To have victory all the day
Knowing He will take care of all our needs
If we'll only follow wherever He leads
With a pure heart, turned toward the One
Who gave us life through His only Son
Through fellowship we know He's there
And all our burdens He'll bear
Just trust in Him and you'll see
Only then will you truly be free
For the road to destruction is wide
It's in Christ that we all must abide

THANK YOU, JESUS

Lord Jesus, I thank you for being in my life
For taking away all the heartache and strife
In a world filled with darkness, evil, and doubt
You've shown me your someone I can't do without
How sad it is when I look all around
So many foundations on sinking ground
But you've shown me the way that I should walk
My foundation's built on you, my rock
While Satan's at work wherever I look
Watching the news, another life that he took
But through it all, you have given me peace
And from all evil ways, with you there's release
So I pray for the world that is blinded and lost
Like an angry ocean, to and fro they are tossed
That's why I thank you, Jesus, all day long
You keep me stable, steadfast, and strong

A MOTHER'S LOVE

A mother's love comes in many ways
It touches our life all our days
It's passed on for generations. It makes us strong
A mother's love is there all our life long
It comes to us daily and in many forms
It comes from other people and out of the norm
Sometimes it's an ear when we need to be heard
A mother's silent love, never speaking a word
Sometimes a mother's love is just a warm embrace
The warmth of her arms puts a smile on our face
Sometimes a mother's love is wisdom to our soul
Her loving advice when life gets out of control
Sometimes a mother's love comes through nurture and teaching
It understands future generations that it will be reaching
Sometimes a mother's love is an encouraging word
That finds a home in our heart, forever to be heard
Sometimes a mother's love doesn't feel like love at all
And it's a love that we don't like when discipline comes to call
A mother's love is special, and it comes in many ways
It comes through various women, who mold us throughout our days
A mother's love doesn't always mean that you have given birth
For a mother's love is simply the Father's love, through women here
on earth

WE ALL USED TO KNOW

What has happened to the life we used to know?
Where we all understood it's by His grace that we go
When life for us wasn't such a rush
We had time for a kind word and a gentle touch
Bring us back to what we all used to know
Bring us back to the place where our hearts would forgive
Without hatred and grudges, in love we would live
When patience and kindness were the order of the day
We were ladies and gentlemen, come what may
Bring us back to what we all used to know
Bring us back to true care and concern for each other
Where we put others first and loved one another
Where we gave and not took and didn't think "we deserve"
But looked for ways to help others and were glad to serve
Bring us back to what we all used to know
Bring us back, Lord, to a place of tears and sorrow
If that's what will bring us a better tomorrow
Bring us back to the things that brought us to our knees
So once again your truth is all that we see
Bring us back to what we all used to know

HIS VICTORY

I know God has worked it together for good
His glorious works have yet to be seen
Everything coming to pass just as it should
Doesn't change all the hurt in between
Yet I thank Him for pain that strengthens my faith
As He brings me along day by day
And I know that it's only because of His grace
I am victorious in every way

NOT MAN'S WAY

To hide behind good is not enough
We must proclaim Christ when the going gets tough
To hide behind love is not the way
For Jesus is love, the Bible does say
Oh, the effort of self that we display
When clearly Jesus said, "I am the way"
In our own strength how we put up a fight
When it's not by our own power or might
Our acts of kindness, though right, won't save
It's salvation to receive, not how we behave
Day after day, our own efforts we render
When Jesus calls us to simply surrender
It is nothing we do of our own merit
But by His grace, to walk in the Spirit

Your Choice

Darkness and light, God's Word makes it clear
There is no in-between when Satan is near
Truth and lies, in God's Word you can see
If you don't believe Christ, you believe the enemy
Chaos and peace, in God's Word you can find
He comforts the heart and supplies rest for the mind
Death and life, in God's Word you can choose
It is life eternal, or it's your soul that you'll lose

OUR WORDS

What does become of the words you say?
Do they bring blessing or pain each day?
And do you use them to edify?
Or are they used to make one cry?
Do they cut to the core like a venomous bite?
Or are they uplifting and shining Christ's light?
Do the words that you say have to build up your pride
Temporarily masking what's wrong inside?
We must think about the words that we say
And use them in love to show others the way

ANGELS CRY

Whenever it rains, I don't know why
I can't help but think the angels cry
The sky, it opens, and down the tears fall
I wonder do they cry for us all
Are their tears from the heartache that they must feel
When they see men lie and cheat and steal?
Or maybe they fall from the greed we can't hide
Or the selfishness that's deep down inside
Do they fall from the wicked words we speak
When God has told us to turn our cheek?
Are they falling for that abusive mate
Or that hand of violence that chose a child's fate?
Are they falling because of drug abuse
As we turn from reality with another excuse?
Or maybe they fall for the ones who must drink
So clouded from alcohol they can't even think
Perhaps they fall when a man works too much
And a wife or a child longs for his touch
Or maybe they fall for what we have made sex
All the pregnancies and diseases that make our lives a wreck
It must break their hearts to see all our pains
I understand the angels' tears, whenever it rains

IT MATTERS

When you need to understand what you don't understand
You're left alone to face the things that you can't face
You need only take His hand and look through His eyes of grace
When the pain is deep inside you and you've let the wrong things guide you
And every day becomes a fight—you just can't seem to get it right
When it doesn't seem to matter and all your prayers have turned to tears
Open His Word and know it matters, as the light dispels your fears

AS IF

It's as if my heart had been packed away
The world punctures it continuously day by day
But the puncture wounds don't seem to bleed
Through them, the Holy Spirit enters, wanting to lead
It's as if my mind had been made clear
No worldly thoughts are welcome there
My soul, the world tried every way to invade it
But it responds to my Lord, the One who created it
It's as if the world tried to steal His glory
But no one can ever change Jesus's story
So come what may, through all my days
Only to Jesus do I give my praise
It's as if the world wanted to crush my spirit
But, Jesus, you're stronger every time the world comes near it
As You faithfully guide and lead my way
For the world to know You, I humbly pray
As hard as it is, I have to say
It's as if it was meant to be this way

WHILE I'M WAITING

Sometimes I sit and can only cry
Sometimes I just want to ask "Why?"
It's then I remember He holds the hurt in my soul
As I hear Jesus say, "I'm in control"
I won't ask why, for the question, you see
Isn't "Why me, Lord?" It is "Why not me?"
He knows better than I ever could
As I wait for Him to work things out for my good
And I'll stand in faith till the day that I die
Confident in Christ, no, I won't ask why

BE CAREFUL

We must be careful what we read
Or on what our hearts and minds do feed
We must be careful what we see
Visions forever can hide within thee
We must be careful what we hear
Don't let the enemy bring despair
We must be careful what we speak
For from our hearts our words do leak
Let truth and righteousness reign in thee
For then the enemy has to flee
Let Christ's love be your guiding light
That others may come to know what's right
We have a choice, truth or sin
It forms our path from deep within
What is the path you walk today?
At the end of it all, what will Christ say?

TRUE CHRISTMAS

He came as a baby, so meek and so mild
Born in a manger, heaven's child
Soon everyone would know that baby's voice
The Savior was born. The world would rejoice
Shepherds and wise men all came from afar
To see the Messiah as they followed a star
With anticipation, the world did await
The newness of life came down from heaven's gate
The hope that was given is hope for all men
The hope from the Father, to give us hope again
He would be the payment for all our sin
With His birth that Christmas, we could all enter in
We could now enter a place like no other
Sins washed away, reconciled to the Father
Who could have known a debt that we couldn't pay
And everything we'd ever need lay right there on the hay?
Who could have known the suffering He'd endure
A birth and a death, to make your salvation sure?
And that is your Christmas—everything you'll ever need
The promise of heaven need only be received
Joy to the world, Emanuel, God with us
He is still within our hearts—Jesus is our Merry Christmas

TRUTHTICIANS

We need "truthticians," not politicians
We need to be biblically, not politically, correct
We need to take a stand, not bow to Satan's hand
We need to follow Jesus's reign, not point and place the blame
We need to yield our authority as unto the Lord
Stand with our country in one accord
Be the authority of salt and light to the earth
Reign from eternal, not political worth
When our authority is all submitted to the Lord
We will truly understand what we're here for
To lead people not to temporal things
But straight to the Lord, Jesus, the King
Salvation the reason and forever will be
Then blessed again will we see our country
Our flag and our freedom, let God know we need Him
Let America proclaim only Jesus's name
And bring the truth into our land again

PURE THOUGHT

Sin, it comes in every color
In every flesh, a sinful dweller
Jesus came to wash our sin
His Holy Spirit now within
The world, it tries to lead the mind
Into sin of every kind
But Jesus paid the sacrifice
In us the mind of Jesus Christ
So thoughts would be of light and pure
The darkness has a place no more
The lies of Satan, we can bind
For Jesus gives us all sound mind

LIFE'S INTERRUPTIONS

When life gets interrupted and the interruptions from the Lord
May we be so quick to listen, for then shall come an important word
Perhaps a word of wisdom, perhaps an answered prayer
Often a blessing in disguise, do we find waiting there
And often in our brokenness, the Lord will give us growth
He gives us strength or gives us healing—sometimes He gives us both
He does this for His purposes that we not remain the same
But go forth useful for His kingdom, to bring Him glory in Jesus's name
His timing, it is perfect, but we often have to wait
Then in these interruptions, Jesus brings forth something great

MUSTARD SEED FAITH

Oh, to have a mustard seed
The smallest of them all
To grow into the strongest faith
When trouble comes to call
Protected in the branches
When the storms of life do beat
A faith that's grounded in the truth
And doesn't know defeat
Jesus said this faith will move
The mountains in our way
But you must learn to never doubt
What God has come to say
The world, it beats to many things
That God says just aren't so
But if you feed your mustard seed
The truth in you will grow
It will get shaken, tossed around, battered, torn, and bruised
But that mustard seed planted in good ground
With Jesus, you can't lose

FERVENT PRAYERS

Listen up. I've got something to say
A little something about how we should pray
God says, "Trade those wishes for fervent prayer
I'm abundantly able. There's no wishing here
If you're wondering why your prayers aren't answered today
Because I want you to remove all the doubt in your way
And when you pray, why do you pray in fear?
Just pray in Jesus's name. I'm still in control here
Why pray so meek that I barely hear your groan
When I've called you to come boldly to my throne?
Why do you pray as if you didn't deserve much
When I am here to bless you with great kingdom stuff?
You are not called to pray according to your own lusts
But it is in my will that I've called you to trust
When you pray to me, I already know what you need
Don't pray just for yourself, but for others intercede
I am not a distant God who cannot be found
And when you pray in the spirit, you are on holy ground
Now I've taught you my ways—they are pure and true
Run along now, my child. You've got some praying to do"

THE CROSS OF MY HEART

Every morning right from the start
I come to God's Word, and I cross my heart
I receive the victory that comes from the cross
It humbles me and tells my flesh who is boss
It's at the cross that I find my fill
And follow Jesus to walk in God's will
I invite the Holy Spirit to come clean my heart
And rid it of anything that might keep us apart
To fill me anew and afresh for the day
For at the cross I do find my way
If I'm different from the world or seem set apart
I give glory to God—yes, I do cross my heart

THE WATER'S REACH

My chair, it awaits me on the beach
My prayers go beyond the ocean's reach
The sand beneath my feet so warm
Walking toward souls still to be reborn
The water is cool by the ocean's roar
I could sit forever on the shore
The wind, it travels where it will
My thoughts go with it as I'm standing still
I see the waves like the ones Jesus walked on
I think of the storms that He's still to calm
I see waves that Peter didn't trust
To have no doubt, it is a must
The smell of fresh and calm and free
Breathing in the grace along shore and sea
The open sky, breathe in the air
If, for a moment, I've not a care

MAMMON

Impressed by money are many, I'm sure
A strange attraction to a temporary cure
It can buy it, fix it, make it all go away
But as you take your last breath, there is nothing it can say
We've allowed it to master and mold who we are
In the façade and falseness, the monies never far
The favor and the friends, good times unending
And we really are something while doing all the spending
But as we lay our head on the pillow each night
The money in our pocket just doesn't add up right
It doesn't fill the loneliness. It doesn't give us peace
As we strive for more and more of it, the greed just fails to cease
It cannot fill the void that only Jesus fills
There is no eternal value in its ever-fleeting thrills
So let me tell you about the spending that every day I do
I spend my time in God's Word, and Jesus sees me through
The value that I put, I do not put in things
And I don't find security in any earthly kings
My treasures, they are priceless in heaven so secure
As well as my rewards, as I'll rejoice forevermore
The things that I count dear, they're treasured deep within
They were given by my Savior, as I exchanged them for my sin
You see, you cannot serve two masters—it is written and it's true
The money or God's truth, which one will master you?

SIN

Sin, it does not "get along." It comes to lead us into "wrong"
Sin, it leads the heart astray. The widened mind and path it lay
Sin deceives, as to distract. Then unawares it plans attack
Sin a darkened language speaks until destruction is complete
But Jesus came, a light to shine. The sin we see, no longer blind
Jesus washed it all away when sinless blood was shed that day
Our fights not flesh, it's spirit fought, for all the flesh shall come to naught
To fight within the spirit realm, I the vessel, Jesus at the helm

THE SEED

I look around and notice
As the enemy plants another seed
I really needn't worry
Jesus knows what it is I need
The enemy, he truly is
So sly and so deceiving
Only by the truth of God's holy Word
Can you know what you're believing
As the darkness comes to steal my soul
And lead a broken heart astray
I rejoice in Jesus, my solid rock
As He does light my way

WHAT IS IT

What is it that you won't lay down
That will bring about a corruptible crown?
What is it that has taken His place
That leads you astray at the end of your race?
You cannot to heaven earthly treasures bring
What has taken the place of Jesus your King?
What is it that you strive for and hold so dear?
What can't you let go of? What do you fear?
This life has nothing that we should cling to
It's when you let go that the Lord can bring you
He will bring you to a place where you can exchange
That corruptible crown and walk in Jesus's name
To be free of the things that bind your heart
Receive an incorruptible crown and an eternal fresh start

IT'S A HIGH PRICE

What is the price tag of one's soul?
What is the price to give the enemy control?
Will you awaken astounded one day
And ask, "When did I give my soul away?"
Don't you know that your soul has been bought?
Your lifetime battles already been fought?
Not only fought, but it has been won
If you make the choice to receive God's Son
The enemy can never have your soul
He can't overcome the Holy Spirit's control
When saved, you are Holy Spirit-filled
Then it's all to Jesus your soul must yield
Don't give the enemy any leeway
Walk with Jesus and live the free way

DENY THE FLESH

What a blessing to hold your peace
To make the fleshly anger cease
To humbly turn the other cheek
Ne'er a cruel word do you speak
To let the Holy Spirit rise
When flesh is screaming otherwise
To kindle with love the flames of sin
To walk away, not enter in
To call upon the name of Jesus
Rather than doing as one pleases
That all might see you, Lord, not me
Now, that, my friend, is what I call free

UNDER GOD

God gave us choice, I am here to say
Who is government to take that away?
As if we knew better or as if we created man
Or as if our politics were better than God's plan
God created us different, our languages and land
He gave us different countries, all made by His hand
He gave us traditions, culture, and ways
And He gave us His Word so we'd all know what He says
If He wanted one world, He'd have made it that way
He said, "Go out into all the world and tell them what I say"
Jesus doesn't change according to what we believe
Jesus is the truth the Father wants us to receive
Make no mistake—only His kingdom will stand
And only those who made the choice to take hold of His hand
It matters not what we think among all our wars and fights
Jesus is calling all of us. He's The Way, The Truth, The Life

Not About Us

It's not about our good
Jesus gave his best
Lay down your weary self
And enter into His rest
It's not about our works
There's nothing we can do
Outstretched arms, nail-scarred hands
Have done it all for you
It's not our holiness
That enables us to enter in
But the holiness of Jesus's blood
That's washed away our sin
What we are or aren't admitting
There is nothing that is hidden
God's Word is eternally settled
It's all because it is written

MORE TIME

How is it that we can think we're wise
As we look around through plank-filled eyes?
That of ourselves we'd have all we need
When the Word of God tells us to take heed?
How is it that we think we're smart?
What truly is it in our heart?
While chasing sin, our energies spent
For the Word of God says to be content
Why is it we've all gone astray
When Jesus said, "I am the way"?
We live our lives as if all was grand
Building on that sinking sand
God's Word reveals how we should walk
And how to build on solid rock
Seems we have so much to learn
More time and grace, Lord, before your return

A HELPING OF THE HOLY SPIRIT

I listen for that still small voice
To guide me as I make a food choice
That healthy things I'd choose to eat
To walk in victory, not defeat
The flesh wants to be satisfied
But Jesus said, "To flesh I've died
Obey my Holy Spirit within
Depend on me if you want to be thin
I nailed your failures to that tree
And rose to give you victory
Now you may think that I don't care
About your plate and what's on there
I want you healthy and physically fit
A purpose for your life that you'd walk in it
That in every area you'd be whole and well
And in your healthy temple I shall dwell"

WHAT IS TOO EXTREME

As I sit and wonder, *What is too extreme?*
And when it comes to Jesus, what exactly do they mean?
As foul language flies out of one's mouth
And cussing does easily flow
That to me is quite extreme, but do they even know?
And what about the drinking? In a drunken stupor state
Get in your car and drive home. Death might be one's fate
Yes, alcohol and drugs night after night
Now isn't that extreme?
But they can't see that picture. They don't understand what I mean
And shall we mention sex, multiple partners in a team?
Girls with girls, guys with guys, now isn't that extreme?
And what about the money? It just never is enough
How extreme is it, when their god has become their stuff?
So tell me exactly why it is that you call me extreme
Hard as I try, I just don't see what you could even mean
And I don't think on judgment day as I stand before the Lord
That I will have to worry about *extreme* even being a word
I cannot picture Jesus saying, "Your heart and mind are just too clean
As I watched you live your life on earth, toward me, you were too
extreme"

STRONGER

With Jesus standing in my defense
I pray for His spirit of excellence
I ask Him, "Lord, what sayest Thou"
I am waiting for your answer now
I prepare for a fast to deny my flesh
To put all my worldly ways to rest
To draw ever near, I won't wait any longer
That your Holy Spirit in me would be stronger

His Friend

Jesus came so that I could be saved
From birth, the road to Calvary paved
Perfect and innocent, the babe lying in the hay
And through life to the cross, He would stay that way
No grumbling and complaining, no asking "Why me?"
He loved through it all, saying, "Father, Thy will be"
Knowing from the start what would be journey's end
Though I'm the reason He had to die, He loves and calls me friend

GLORIOUS CHRISTMAS

That glorious Christmas morning
As Mary held him to her breast
Thus began his journey
As God gave us his best
Everything we'd ever need
Came in the flesh that day
Emanuel, God with us, nothing more to say
He came, he healed, he preached, he taught
Died on the cross, our sins blood-bought
Everything that we couldn't be
Led our Christmas to Calvary
Our Counselor and our Prince of peace
The light that makes the darkness cease
Such a glorious holy season
How could we celebrate any other reason
It is not about Santa, as some would say
But the Word made flesh on Christmas Day
So think about that gift as you give and receive
The Father sent his all. Why wouldn't you believe?

BIBLICAL FOUNDATION

I stand with Jesus
And my USA
We believe God's Word
And what the Bible does say
We exult Jesus's name
We lift it on high
Our blessings and freedoms
We know Jesus is why
Everything that we are
Is because of that cross
He came to give life
And to redeem the lost
Jesus is the vine in which we abide
Our flag, our freedoms
And Jesus by our side

FREEDOM IN CHRIST

Jesus, I pray for those who just don't see
That only in Christ can we truly be free
That you have broken the chains that bind
Emotionally, physically, and in our minds
Your ways are good and right and true
And to get to the Father we must come through You
We must stand firm and boldly proclaim
There isn't forgiveness in any other name
You call each one to make that choice
If we'd only respond to that still small voice
We'd be delivered from the sins that bind
True freedom in Jesus is what we will find

LET IT GO

Everything that we hold dear
Will surely one day disappear
What in this life did you behold
That was worth trading for streets of gold
What did you cling to, what earthly thing
Was worth trading for your heavenly King
What was it you found so much that pleases
That was worth denying your Lord Jesus
When that day comes you'll stand to find
It's far too late to change your mind
You've made a choice and traded your soul
For a life on earth you thought you'd control
Now that path you took, you find it to be
Separation from God through through eternity
For there is no second chance; after death you will say
As your knee does bow, "Jesus you are The Way"

HOW GREAT THOU ART

I would like you to meet my friend Art
He's often very quiet and can be very smart
He is always with me but also everywhere
And even though you see him, you'd never know he's there
I can see him high. I can see him low
I teach him to praise Jesus everywhere I go
The beauty that Art creates, it just doesn't compare
To the beauty of the cross and what was created there
Some days Art is good, and some days Art is bad
Some days I rejoice with Art. Some days he makes me mad
And though Art is a friend like no other
Jesus, my truest friend, sticks closer than a brother
Art is always here, and although he's very fun
Truly I must let all know, "Jesus, Thou art the saving One"

I Am Still "I Am"

A broken angel, the most beautiful kind
It's amazing what in Jesus, in brokenness, one does find
It's in our brokenness when we feel of no use
That Jesus brings forth his glorious truth
From the ashes of pain, only Jesus can bring forth
Kingdom purposes and a life of true worth
When on our own, we are left with the pieces
Self has been shattered. Thus, His Spirit increases
Jesus lifts us up to stand tall and true
As He says, "Don't you know what I've done for you?
I was broken so that you would not be
I was nailed to the cross so that you could be free
Crucified and buried, put in the ground
But risen for you that you won't be bound
Know that your brokenness is a lie—it's not truth
Not when the power of my blood covers you
Now arise and go forth, in the power of my name
And let all the world know the reason I came
Live my Word. Speak my name in every nation
Let them all know I, Jesus, am salvation
Let them know. Tell whomever you can
There will never be another. I am still "I Am"

HE LISTENS

If I listen, I can fly higher, and with a truer voice I sing
Since I've humbly come before the Lord and laid down my broken wing
For my notes are often sour, but when He listens, I have found
Out of tune and though off-key, to Him, there's no sweeter sound
For Jesus doesn't listen as we do with human ear
His ways are far above ours. He has another way to hear
And as our cries ascend to Him, our mess He turns to work of art
It matters not how we might sound, because the Lord, He hears your heart

WHEN IT HURTS

Lord, take my heartache
The heaviness of my days
When sadness comes in
Teach me to turn it into praise
When the hurt of this life
On my shoulders does rest
May my thoughts be eternal
And of how I am blessed
For I know that you hold
Each tear that I cry
When I don't understand
The how, when, or why
Only you ease the pain
Only you bring true healing
And in Jesus's name I am grateful
No matter what I am feeling
Help me to remember
I am blessed beyond measure
May my focus be of You, Lord
And in heaven be my treasure

THIS IS EASTER

The unrefutable empty grave
A risen Savior who came to save
No epitaph does His tombstone hold
But the way that eternity would unfold
No flowers to change each holiday
But His Holy Spirit to guide the way
No tears because we won't see Him again
But a brother who sticks closer than a friend
No dates to reveal a limited life span
But the Alpha and Omega, the great I Am
No regrets about what we didn't say
But His voice tells us, "I am the way"
No tomorrows for missing the one who's not here
But every new day, a chance to draw near
No praying at His grave, wondering if He'll hear
But the way for our praying, through Him, it's made clear
Not bound by a coffin, no ashes strewn about
But a stone rolled away—"He's not here" was the shout
Come to the empty tomb and be filled today
Through His death we have life—that's what Easter does say

A Dreamer

Maybe I'm a dreamer
And no one dreams the way I do
Even though I am a dreamer
I still believe that dreams come true
I don't dream of things
No big fine house
Not some fancy car
I don't ask for things
Not even little things
Don't wish upon a star
'Cause things will never satisfy
The yearning in my heart
I yearn for truth, eternal things
And the enemy to depart

PITTSBURGH MORNING RUN

The fall morning weather
So crisp and so clean
Summer and winter
I'm now in between
The leaves, oh the colors
They take my breath away
The handiwork of God
Leaves me much to say
A cleansing for the eye
That knows the hand of truth
Give glory to His name
Is all that I can do
Refreshing to the soul
Yes, a sight to behold
To see the wonders of His majesty
It never does grow old
I'm taken by the beauty
The treasures of His hand
As I'm learning to see Jesus
All across this land

HARDEN NOT YOUR HEART

When there is hardness in your heart
It keeps the Lord and you apart
The closeness that He wants to share
Is kept away by sin that's there
When one is bitter and cannot forgive
One cannot in His fullness live
When unforgiveness takes its place
It stands against the Savior's grace
When hate is there instead of love
It hinders blessings from above
The enemy wants to steal your heart
And piece by piece tear it apart
To fill it with his twisted ways
To keep you from all that Jesus says
Jesus says to search your heart
And let no lie keep you apart
From what is written and what is true
And all that He wants to do in you
Surrender what has held you back
Take victory over the enemy's attack
Jesus calls you to a fresh start
Hear Him and harden not your heart

THE GIFT

The Father said, "Beware of danger
True peace is only found in that manger
Don't you listen to the voice of a stranger
I've laid the voice of truth in that manger
I sent salvation that Christmas Day
For a lost world to know the way
No room for a history re-arranger
The beginning and end is found in that manger
No other place did I lay my Son
To come to Me, He is the One
You can't change God's Word
As man does as he pleases
The living Word in a manger
And His name is Jesus
You can fight if you must—I gave you that will
Deny His name, but He is Jesus still
And He calls you right now as the world goes adrift
Receive in your heart Jesus, my gift"

TIME TO RISE

Wake up and rise up to stand in truth
To proclaim the name of Jesus, we must do what we must do
Don't be intimidated or let the evil plans unfold
We're called to speak the truth in love and Jesus's name proclaims it
bold
We have all the victory of His resurrection power
And greater things will we do until that coming hour
Let the sick be healed, the lost be found, the captives all set free
Tell the world and everyone you know what He's done for you and
me
There's no time to wonder. There's no place for doubt
Go and tell everyone you can what Jesus is about
He'll change your life. He'll right your wrong and truly set you free
He'll pull you from the enemy's fire into the light of eternity

SALVATION'S CALL

What is the message of the church today?
When so many are being led astray
Are you listening to hear God's truth
And what Jesus Christ has done for you?
Are you hearing that He still calls "Come"?
It doesn't matter who you are or what you have done
No matter the sin, you can lay it down
Confess, repent, and pick up your crown
There is no judgment or guilt or shame
It's all nailed to the cross, in Jesus's name
There are no buts, no ifs, or I-don't-understands
Jesus says, "Lay it all down and come take my hand
I've come to rid you of every doubt, every fear
I died and rose for you. Your victory is here
Come take a stand for Me. I won't let you fall
I've paid your sin debt. You are free from it all
As the day draws near, tribulations shall rise
The worldly chaos should be no surprise
But the truth that I Am will see you through it all
Make that choice. Hear the truth
Answer salvation's call"

THE STORY

Change is coming—yes, indeed
As the Holy Spirit fills our need
Bringing salvation to the lost
Revealing truth by the light of the cross
So no matter how dark the darkness can be
Jesus shines brighter—He is victory
Defeating the lies and the enemy's hold
As truth rises up, Jesus's story unfolds

MASTERPIECE

Be for Jesus a work of art
Shine His light into the dark
Tell the world what Jesus is about
A light no way an enemy can put out
Sing of Jesus's truth and grace
Salvation for the whole human race
For God so loved, we must understand
Jesus is calling—won't you take His hand?
There is no other way, you see
Jesus is the Father's eternity
He calls you now to make that choice
As to Jesus, lift up your voice
Surrender your heart. Receive what He gives
To self we die; to Jesus we live
Receive or reject is all we must do
The choice is yours for Jesus loves you

YEAH...BUT

I do not want a faith of "yeah...but"
Where the enemy keeps me in a doubting rut
But a faith where I can rise and soar
In everything that my Jesus died for
To rise above the pain of earth
To the freedom in our second birth
To rise above the hurt and sorrow
No matter what may come tomorrow
For at this moment we have today
To let others know Jesus is the way
To stand against the world's "Yeah...but"
Tell them Jesus is for sure, no matter what

He Came

He came to die so that we could live
He bore all our sins so that we could forgive
He left His throne knowing what He would face
Taking our guilt to the cross, He died in our place
But that death brought life. Death couldn't hold Him down
A risen Savior, hope for the world was found
Our sin debt has been paid forevermore
And we will find open arms awaiting us at heaven's door

A TRIBUTE TO FIN

Written in honor of my grandfather, Finley James Davis

You left one day so long ago for a war that called your name
How were we to ever know that our lives were forever changed
That you'd not return to the life you left and a wife who loved you so
Or mold and shape your daughter's life and watch her as she'd grow
We remember the day they came to say you'd not be coming home
That you had been captured in the war, your whereabouts unknown
The pain we felt, the disbelief, the sorrow, and the despair
The images that played in our minds of what happened over there
Were you alone? Were you afraid? Did they treat you bad?
Were you worried, full of doubt? Or were you just plain mad?
These are the things we've often thought, over all these years
The answers that we never got brought emptiness and tears
And time went on, our family grew, and stories, they were told
Of a man we loved but never knew, back in the days of old
And now some sixty years have passed, and we have come to find
Our beloved soldier is coming home—you were not left behind
All this time you've been right here, right on our American land
You were not kept from coming home, not by the enemy's hand
And today, at last, you're laid to rest; and Old Glory, she still waves
Because *you*, our soldier, gave his best, so valiant and so brave
We give the glory to *God* after all this time. He has brought this to an end
The closure that has come at last, so that all our hearts can mend
And we salute you, our soldier. Rest in peace. You have done your part
And you will forever live on and on, right here, in all our hearts

No Production

The Christian life is not an act
It is living God's Word, absolute fact
The Christian life is not a play
That needs applause at the end of the day
The Christian life has no rehearsed line
But words spoken of Holy Spirit divine
The Christian life doesn't have different scenes
For Christ doesn't change according to dreams
We don't look for trophies made by man
We'll receive a gold crown for the race we've ran
There is no box office or tickets to buy
It's all given freely—that's why Christ did die
In the Christian life when your curtain goes down
Not a stage, but on solid rock you'll be found

PRAISE HIM

Jesus, I praise you
With all my heart I do
I rejoice and stand before you
Captivated by your truth
The freedom that I walk in
Is a treasure to behold
I know it won't compare to
When I walk on streets of gold
I'm an heir and a joint heir
To the sovereign King of kings
What a healing and a strength
That only your name brings

A SUPPORT SYSTEM OF LOVE

A support system of love
Was given to everyone
It started with the Father
Was passed down through the Son
Jesus lived and walked it
In His time upon this earth
He gave it as He taught us
Of life and second birth
He loved as He was beaten
To the cross our shame He wore
He loved us as they pierced His side
He loved all the way to death's door
He loved us as we mocked Him
His love never spoke a word
But through His silent suffering
Love was all we heard
He loved us to the grave
As His body they laid to rest
A love unlike no other
Our God, He gave His best
His love so overwhelming
In the grave it could not stay
A love so true and powerful
The stone was rolled away
They say that love can change the world
Well, it did, as it hung upon that tree
His love changes life upon this earth
And through all eternity

CHRISTMAS MEANS

C is for when He Came into the world, our souls to save
H is for the Healing flowing from His stripes that day
R is for Redemption that comes in no other name
I is for "In Christ." It's there you'll never be the same
S is for the Savior who came to set us free
T is for Transgressions, ours that He nailed upon that tree
M is for the Mercy so that our guilt we do not bare
A is for Ascension as He went a place for us to prepare
S is So you know that He came from above

Christ is Christmas, the Father's perfect gift of love

JESUS SAID

This is my body given for you
As I watch from above to see what you do
I was poured out to forgive your sin
Why do you hesitate to enter in?
I tell you the truth—I am life everlasting
All that I am is yours for the asking
Why do you not eat of this bread
But look to be filled from the world instead?
I gave my all that you'd be made new
My death and resurrection is forgiveness for you
Don't you know when you eat the world's bread
It brings death and destruction instead?
I've called you to drink of the fruit of this vine
The Father's plan, He made it mine
He sent me here as eternal bread
For in your sin, you'd be left dead
Rise with me and eat of your fill
I am your Savior, God's perfect will

CAREFULLY IN TUNE

Be careful of the words on which your eyes and mind do feed
For the enemy has a melody and his tune is to deceive
He sings of love for he does know it's something we all need
If it's not the love that Jesus speaks, he is planting enemy seeds
He will even sing about a god but not the Godhead, three in one
He sings about a different god, not Jesus, Savior, Son
And hurting hearts would sing along and never think it twice
But I am singing Jesus's song, and this is my advice
It doesn't matter what the beat or what awesome notes you've heard
Don't sing along with every tune if it doesn't line with God's Word
For every song is sung by one who has a story to sell
And there is a god it sings of, and this is how you tell
Does it glorify the things of Christ? Is Jesus lifted high?
Or is it vaguely generalized, as the darkness slips it by?
For through the music the enemy's learned to slowly gain control
My friend, it isn't about the tune at all. No, it's about your soul

Song of the Spirit

The words, they cover you like a disguise
And the story in your song is no surprise
Your notes flow freely, music to my ear
And the love that it sends, no one else can hear
Your tune, it comes to me and it captures my soul
And it wraps around my heart until it's out of control
The lyrics, they enter the depths of my being
And only I understand what it is I am seeing
I am seeing and hearing the beat that you play
And my heart is in tune with the words you can't say

FIRM IN CHRIST

I see the world in pain and distress
But in Christ you can find peace and rest
Do not be tossed by circumstance
But be firm in His unchanging hand
In Christ you can be worry-free
Walking in His victory
Applying His truth come what may
His Holy Spirit to lead the way
It matters not what the world does say
Trust in Jesus day by day

DAILY ATTACKS

Day by day in the enemy's attack
I still praise Jesus. He's got my back
I won't forsake the only God I serve
I will give Him the praise He alone deserves
No matter what tribulation may bring
I will still give the glory to Jesus my King
For there is no other—it's in Christ alone I trust
He is Savior, Redeemer. He is righteous, true, and just

HOLY WEEK

As I think of the circumstances of this holy week
To understand that my God is what I seek
I can't imagine what was heavier, the cross that He bore
Or the burden from the weight of my sin that He wore
I can't imagine the thoughts that went through His mind
Just knowing that His thoughts are so much higher than mine
As I think of the weariness in His physical being
I think of the strength that the world wasn't seeing
I think of the love, the reason He endured
And His blood that was shed so that I would be cured
I think of Him never even uttering a sound
The silence that ensured that the lost would be found
As I ponder Calvary's path this holy week
Do I know for certain whom it is I seek?

Pour Down Your Reign

The rain came down good and hard
As it watered everything in my backyard
The hard dry ground sure helped me see
How much, Lord, I need you to reign in me
When the first drops fell and bounced off the dirt
It was like my hardened heart from all life's hurt
As the rain kept falling, steady and sure
The ground began to soften as the earth yearned for more
And over time, my heart drenched in truth
Began to soften as you reign in me too
And what was once so dry, parched, and hardened
Has blossomed like a well-watered garden
Bringing forth life and fruit for each season
A well-watered ground being the reason
Strong roots take hold as I'm grounded in you
I produce things now that are good and true
I can then in others plant a seed
Yes, Lord, come and reign in me, indeed

THE ENEMY WILL FLEE

Evil can't have any more power than you give it
Evil can't stay if you refuse to live it
Glory to God, our battles already won
We can now walk in the power of His Son
The grave is empty, and the victory is written
So stand in Jesus when you feel like quitting
There is no reason to stand in another place
Jesus gave you His all no matter what you face
Remember the enemy, that he is a liar
Jesus the truth, to rise so much higher
Who are you giving the victory to today
Claim the blood of Jesus, and from the enemy walk away

EASTER BASKET

We celebrate Easter but once a year
A risen Savior, the Father's love comes near
So here's my question, and I have to ask it
What's truly inside of your Easter basket?
Is it chocolates, candies, eggs, and such?
Perhaps we treat it like Jesus—I'll have a little but not too much
Do you bring out your basket and put it on display
But then, like Jesus, the rest of the year it's put away?
Do you go to church in your Sunday's best
But, the remainder of the year, on Sundays you rest?
Perhaps you partake in an Easter egg hunt
With Jesus on the back burner, little kids up front
Maybe you'll gather with your family for dinner
Even mumble a prayer, giving thanks as a sinner
Well, I want you to picture your Easter basket
Now, Jesus's cold tomb, not some fancy casket
Resurrected for us, paid our sin debt in full
For He knew how our lives would get out of control
Yet with forgiveness, compassion, and arms open wide
The door is still open. He invites you inside
To partake in life, and it's life everlasting
He'll come into your heart if you'll only ask Him
A Savior who awaits, He died that we might live
Making a way to the Father, eternal life He does give
So as you think about Easter, do you really know the story?
It's the Father, Holy Spirit, Son, resurrected in all His glory

CHRISTMAS LETTER TO JESUS

You have filled my heart with love and truth
Christmas Day, it is my living proof
You came to earth to pay my debt
I haven't fully understood that yet
But every day my heart is filled
With the truth that through you the Father willed
I am filled with joy and love and peace
A blessed assurance that doesn't cease
A calm within, of soul and mind
The calm longing hearts are searching to find
A gift that was given for all eternity
A baby in a manger that came to save me

WHAT IS YOUR CHRISTMAS?

What does Christmas mean to you?
Is it shopping, decorating, and too much to do?
Is it hustle and bustle and rushing around?
Is it fretting and worry, no peace to be found?
Is it Santa and family or being kind to a stranger
But never a thought of that gift in a manger?
Is it malls and stores with deals that can't be beat?
Do you end up a Martha or a Mary at Jesus's feet?
Is it cooking and cleaning as you try to impress?
Is your focus on the Savior or the commercialized mess?
Does the music that you choose tell the real Christmas story?
Or are you drawn to the chaos as the world steals God's glory?
Did you stop to remember you're the reason that He came?
Are you truly aware that Christmas has a name?
It is Jesus, our Savior, the birth of our Lord
He is Christmas, your gift, the Father's living Word

HOW I SEE CHRISTMAS

When I look at Christmas lights, the story is told
Because they remind me He's the light of the world
When I hear Christmas carols, it becomes so clear
To bring us salvation is why He came near
When I do Christmas shopping and check off my list
It makes me grateful for God's perfect gift
As I decorate and trim my Christmas tree
It reminds me of the bare one that He died on for me
As I gather with loved ones in laughter and fun
I remember that today, He's still rejected by some
This is my Christmas prayer for you this season
That you would know in your heart
Jesus Christ, the true reason

Lord, Please Protect Me

Lord Jesus, protect my ears
From things I don't need to hear
Lord Jesus, protect my sight
From things that block your shining light
Lord Jesus, protect my mind
So that all my thoughts leave the world behind
Lord Jesus, protect my words
So that when I speak, your truth is heard

COMPROMISE

There is no conflict. There is no compromise
Within Jesus our Savior, all-knowing, all-wise
There is no division. There is no contradiction
All that is within our human affliction
There is nothing more certain. There is nothing more sure
Than to know that in Jesus we are eternally secure
He calls us to walk in victory and in truth
His Holy Spirit is with us to see that we do
The enemy will taunt you with all his lies
He'll lead you to live that life of compromise
In Jesus you have truth, and deliverance you will find
Choose to daily walk the Word. Leave your compromise behind

I AM IS COMING

I Am is coming, and what shall He find?
Will you run to His arms or be left behind?
Will you recognize the voice as the one you obeyed?
Or will it sound like thunder and find you afraid?
Will your joy overflow as you cry out "My King"?
Or while here on earth, to false gods did you sing?
Is your robe white as snow from the blood of the Lamb?
Jesus is coming, and you shall see the I Am

CHRISTMAS FOR ALL

At Christmastime as I reflect
The birth of a King whom the world would reject
What is Christmas? Jesus at birth
The Word made flesh, the Father's worth
Christmas is a gift to turn every wrong right
The peace within our hearts became life that silent night
The pain the world had brought, the King would wipe away
And for every lonely heart, love was here to stay
Three wise men brought their gifts, but nothing could compare
To the lowly humble manger with the Savior lying there
The world forever changed with every heartbeat
His life endured our suffering. Through Him, we're made complete
The gift above all gifts, perfect in every way
Reconciliation to the Father, our blessed hope is Christmas Day
So when others are joyful, do not wonder *if*
Come and receive Him for yourself because He is your Christmas gift

OH, TO BE

Oh, to be meek and gentle, like I read about in your Word
Oh, to be able to apply all the gospel truth I've heard
To never give the flesh a place as I press on for my crown
That all would see, as they look at me, the Savior who came down
That the hope that is inside of me would be in every word
That in everything I am and speak, only truth would be what's heard
To shine the light of Jesus just as we're called to do
And in everything about me that light would come shine through
That anyone who looks my way would never have to doubt
Of who I am and whose I am or what I am about
To walk according to his plan each and every day
Walking right through that straight gate where narrow is the way

HE IS CALLING

He is calling us as a country
His Word does make us wise
His blessing awaits
As well as his warning
We must stop the compromise
He gives us the freedom to make our choice
But cautions us not to ignore his voice
His Holy Spirit will lead and guide
But in his Word we must abide
It is for our good, our own well-being
But lately the hand of the enemy we're seeing
We've bought into deception and all his lies
God's spirit is warning it will be our demise
God's Holy Spirit is calling, "Repent and arise"

Do I

Jesus, do I know you?
Or do I just know of you?
Do I truly keep you first
And put no one above you?
Do I long to walk in truth?
Or do I make my own?
Is my life reflecting you?
Do I make my or your name known?
Do others know I'm Christian
By what I say and do?
Do they see in me something different?
Do I tell them that it is you?
Or am I blended in with the world
That you tell me not to be of?
Do they see the world in me?
Or do I truly shine your love?
Have I failed to walk in victory
Your precious resurrection power?
Do I speak and claim your promises
Every day and every hour?
For there is a world that's hurting
They are looking for the truth
Do they see you in me, Jesus?
Is my life truly claiming you?

THE VOICE

A voice does travel wherever it pleases
No way to reach the heavens
But thus through Jesus
In the middle of difficult lies
The truth of Jesus will always rise
If it doesn't, be it understood
The Lord will show you
That you call evil good
Reevaluate the things
To which your heart and mind do cling
For from within shall come
The song your soul will sing
For you cannot hide in words
What it is that you treasure most
Test the spirits Jesus tells us
Of your truth, your life will boast

YA THINK

I think too deep
I think too long
I'm always thinking
Is something wrong?
I think too little
I think too much
Perhaps my thinking is out of touch
I think too fast
I think too slow
I overthink a lot, I know
I think it quick
I think it through
I wonder if you think it too
I think it big
I think it small
I wonder if I should think at all
I think it happy
I think it sad
I can think so hard that I make myself mad
Thoughts can change as quick as a wink
Thoughts are amazing—what do you think?
My mind doesn't think, though, on whatever it pleases
My mind thinks on the things of Jesus

THE FLOWER

Gone from us, you beautiful flower
You left us at the midday hour
Who would have known that before you could bloom
You would choose to leave us so soon?
You were flourishing and growing. You shone like the sun
But deep inside you were a garden of one
We were here to water and watch you grow
Not knowing the weeds that had tangled you so
Beautiful to the eye, a sweet fragrance for all
You were wilting away. Why didn't you call?
We could have dug and fertilized the soil
Loved and nourished you so that you'd never spoil
But we found you there trampled to the ground
Withered and broken, the only flower around
Plucked from this world and our lives too soon
But in our hearts, you'll forever bloom

GIVE THANKS

How easy it is to give thanks when we walk in good health
And easily we give thanks for blessings and our wealth
It is easy to give thanks when everything is good
But do we really give the thanks that we all know we should?
Are we thankful for that worry that kept us awake?
Are we thankful for that burden that caused our hearts to break?
Are we thankful when times get rough
When funds are low and we haven't enough?
Are we thankful when the body's in pain
When we don't understand and things can't be explained?
Are we thankful when we've had enough
When others are weak and we have to be tough?
Are we thankful when everything goes wrong
And we just don't have the will to be strong?
Are we thankful when the tears just fall
And we wonder how we'll get through it all?
When the things of life seem to tear us apart
Is there really thanks in our heart?
Or do we give thanks according to our mood
Picking and choosing the gratitude?
Because we serve a God who gave His all
He laid down His life because of man's fall
His Word says to give thanks in all things
We are called to give thanks in whatever life brings
And we can give thanks, no matter the case
When we understand it's all by His grace
And we can give thanks when nothing seems right
Jesus came to that darkness to turn it to light

And at the cross, He will see you through
No matter what life has brought to you
When you know who it is to whom you give thanks
That will put your gratitude in a whole other rank
So no matter what it is that you may be living
Look to the cross and join me in thanksgiving

UNTIL

I think about everything that Jesus said
And everything that He is, is my living bread
To drink of His cup and eat to my fill
I would walk in the fullness of God's living will
His Holy Spirit subduing my flesh
In His holy presence, I'd walk only blessed
I'll walk this earth my armor intact
Yielded to Jesus until He comes back

YOUR CALVARY

Stuck on the road to Calvary
Can't get to the cross that will set you free
The pain and the burden too heavy to bear
Wondering if anyone would even care
The path so familiar to the steps of our Lord
So broken and beaten, the One we adored
And you find yourself on that well-worn road
Buckling under the weight of your load
As you struggle to hold back another tear
Jesus gently whispers, "I am still here
You are not forgotten, and you are not alone
In all your troubles I am still on the throne
I hear you, I'm near you, and I'll never leave
You've made it to the cross. You need only believe"

MEMORIAL DAY

We are the land of the free and home of the brave
It is under the cross that our flag does wave
There are those who try to push the cross aside
And deny the men and women who for our freedom died
So I stand in defense of those who gave their all
That we not be overtaken or to the enemy our country fall
I honor them today with a heart of gratitude
And for the families that sacrifice in everything they do
And on this Memorial Day I know who the true heroes are
The ones who are and will be and the ones who've gone before

THE FOURTH OF JULY

What was it that was really born on that first fourth of July?
An America and a people free to lift Jesus as Lord on high
Acknowledging our freedoms, we call it Independence Day
Free to think and say and do whatever, come what may
And though that's our independence we the people still freely say
On Jesus, we are dependent still, forever, till our dying day
And our flag stands for that freedom and the many who bravely died
And we won't let the enemy behind our freedoms hide
So I stand here in the truth, in Jesus's name
I stand for our freedoms and our Jesus who came
That we would no longer buy into the lie that America is changing
Or that in vain some did die
Jesus is at the center still, and He has heard our cry
So remember what it truly means when you say
Happy Fourth of July

TRUTH OR LIES

Truth and lies help you realize
What it is that you see
If it is lies, you stay in bondage
If truth, then you are free
The enemy cannot keep you
If you know he doesn't have the power
For his greatest strength was defeated
At Jesus's resurrection hour
For one can only be bound
When remaining in a lie
That you would walk in freedom
Is true power from on high
So the next time you are believing
That the enemy has a hold
Walk away in Jesus's truth
And watch your victory unfold

20/20 Eternal Vision

They tell me that I see the lies
That's only with my earthly eyes
My heart, it has eyes of its own
Eternal truth that will carry me home
My earthly eyes can see with grace
But my heart has eyes that walk by faith
That see beyond the earthly things
The truth that only Jesus brings
My heart, it looks through eyes of love
Spiritual sight from heaven above
The earthly eyes see what's not real
And try to rule the way I feel
My heart has eyes that see what's true
No matter what the world may do
And sight not given by any man
Revealing what only the Holy Spirit can
Jesus wants believers to see
What He died for at Calvary
So looking past the natural eye
You'll see a true vision from on high

About the Author

Robyn Sorensen was born and raised in West Mifflin, Pennsylvania. She has lived in Las Vegas, Nevada, for the past thirty-five years. She loves the Lord, her family, and her country. She enjoys spending time with her family, working out, and the beach. She has been in the service industry for twenty-five years. She loves God's Word and her church family. Robyn has a wonderful husband, a son, and a precious Jack Russell named Mable.

Printed in the USA
CPSIA information can be obtained
at www.ICGtesting.com
CBHW031819261024
16400CB00037B/469